Drawing Super Cute Baby Animals
using Lowercase Letters

Created by STEVE HARPSTER

www.harptoons.com

Copyright © 2016 Steve Harpster
All characters are property of Steve Harpster and Harptoons Publishing
All rights reserved

www.harptoons.com

Harpster, Steve
Drawing Super Cute Baby Animals Using Lowercase Letters/ written and illustrated by Steve Harpster

SUMMARY: Learn how to draw cute baby animals starting with a lowercase letter
ART / General, JUVENILE FICTION / General

ISBN 13: 978-0-9960197-6-7
ISBN 10: 0-9960197-6-6

SAN: 859-6921

To my wife Karen. Thank you for your help and support in making Harptoons a reality and a success.

Follow Harptoons on:

For school visit information
www.harptoons.com or
contact Steve Harpster at
steve@harptoons.com

Andy Alligator

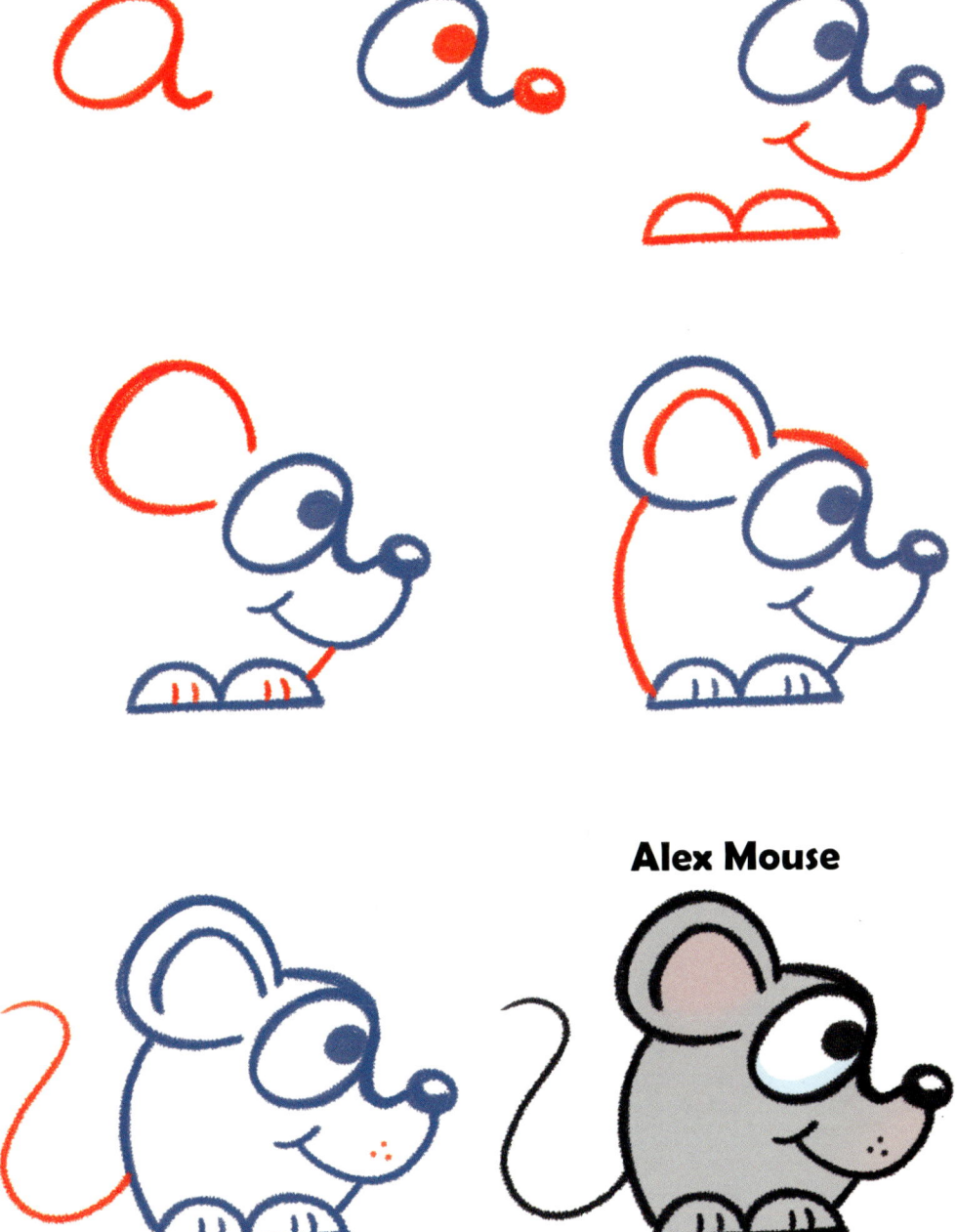
Alex Mouse

Betty Bunny

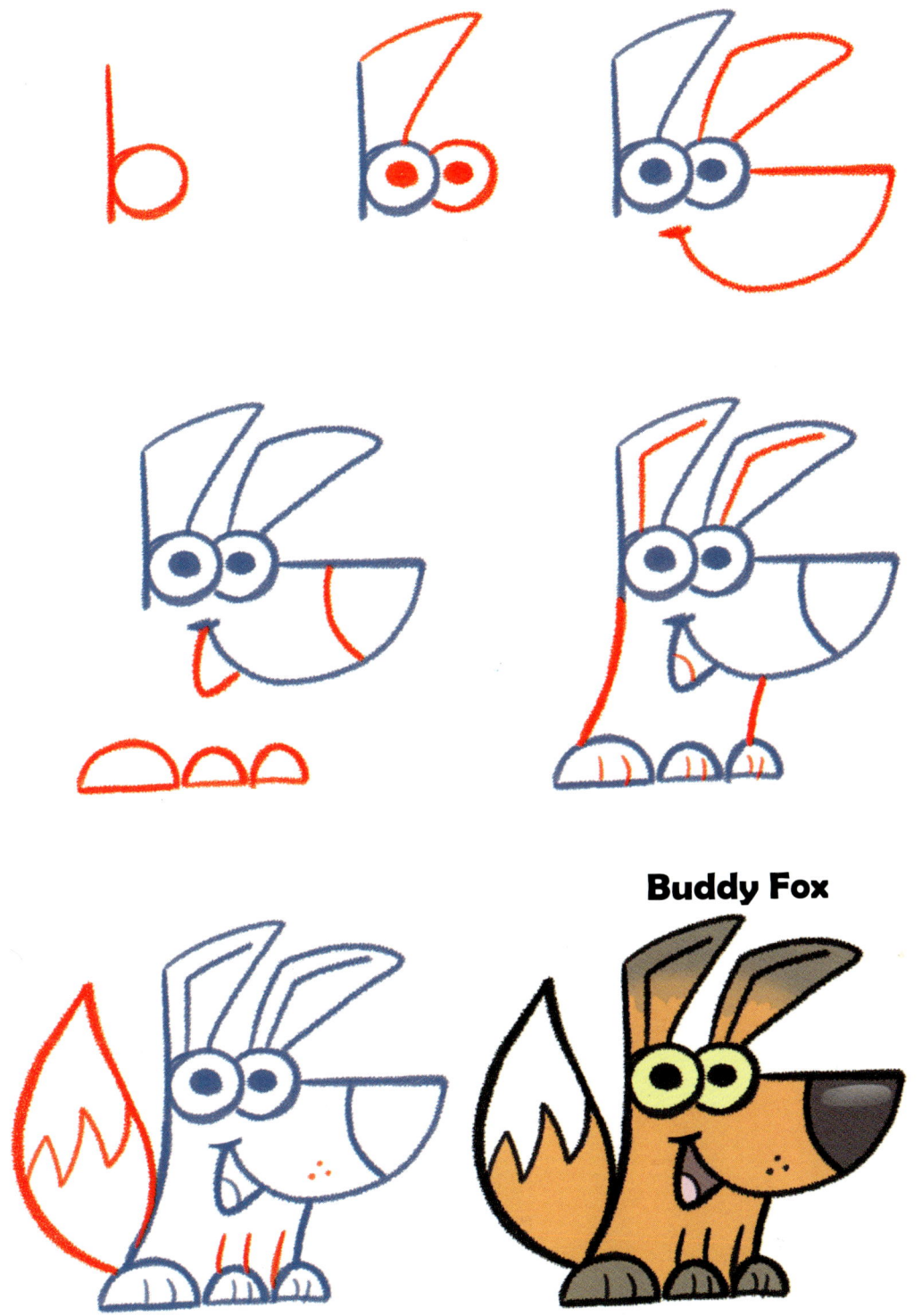

Buddy Fox

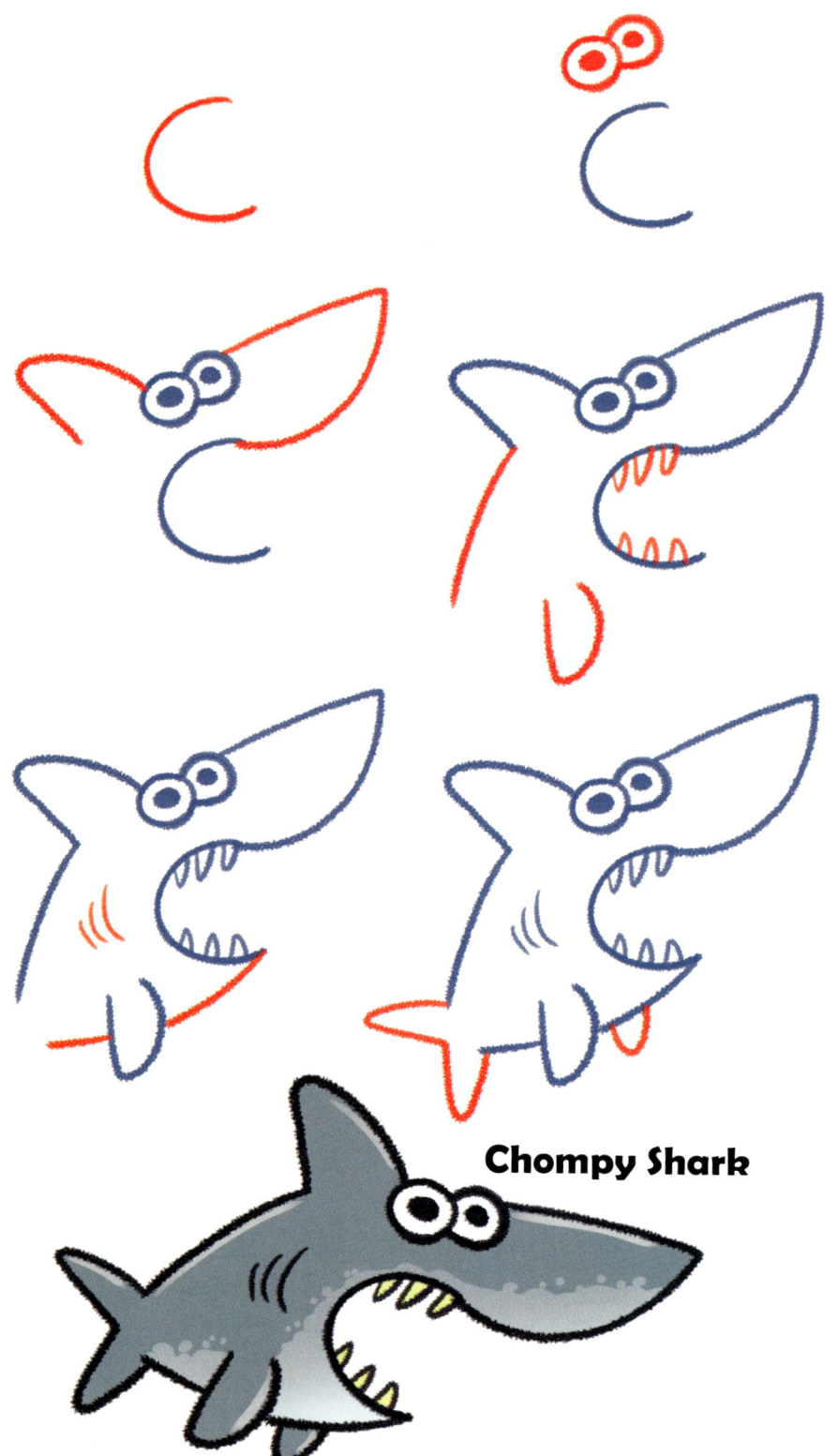

Chompy Shark

Charlie Guinea Pig

Daisy Dog

Frank Koala

Garrett Tiger

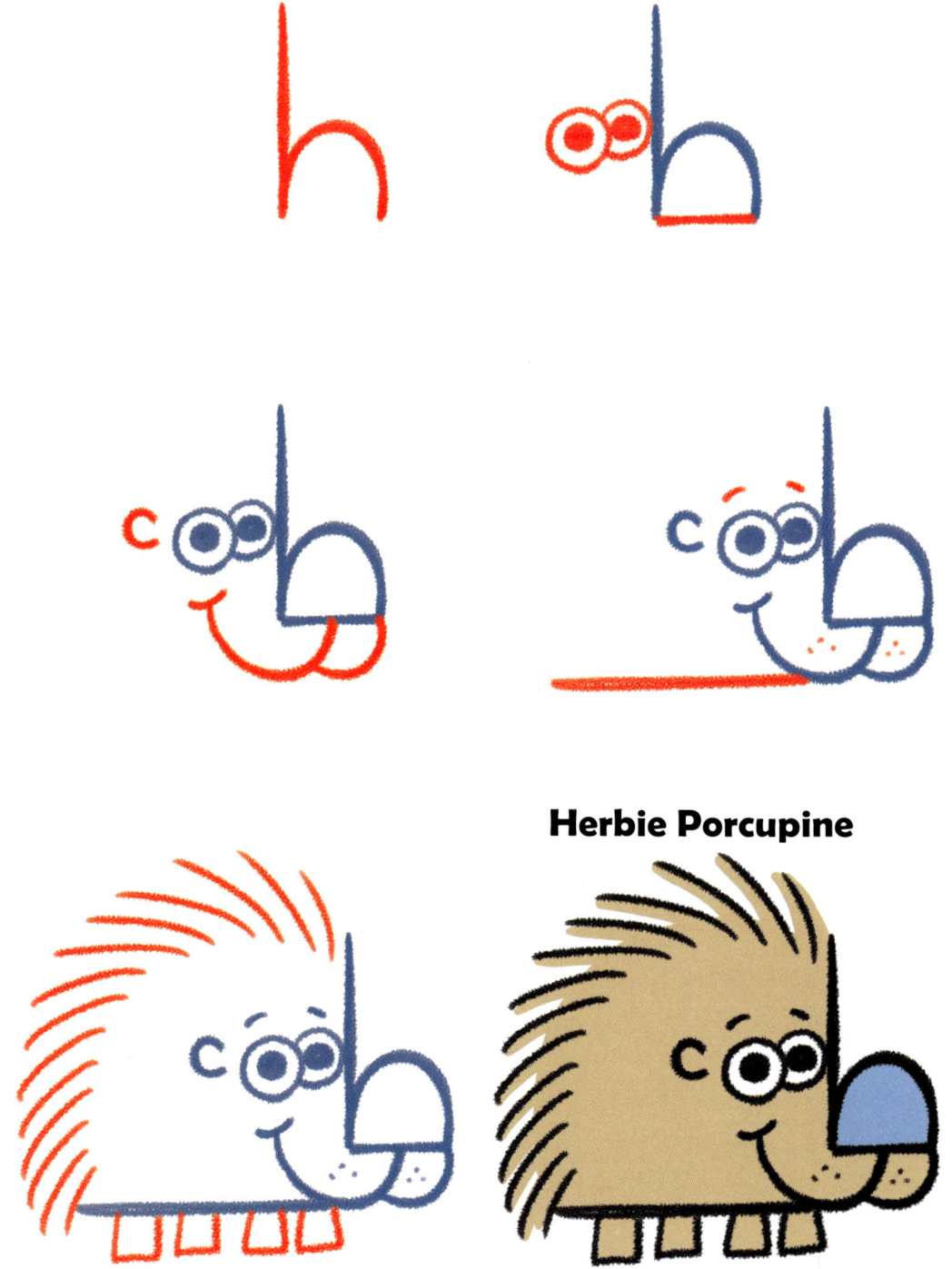

Herbie Porcupine

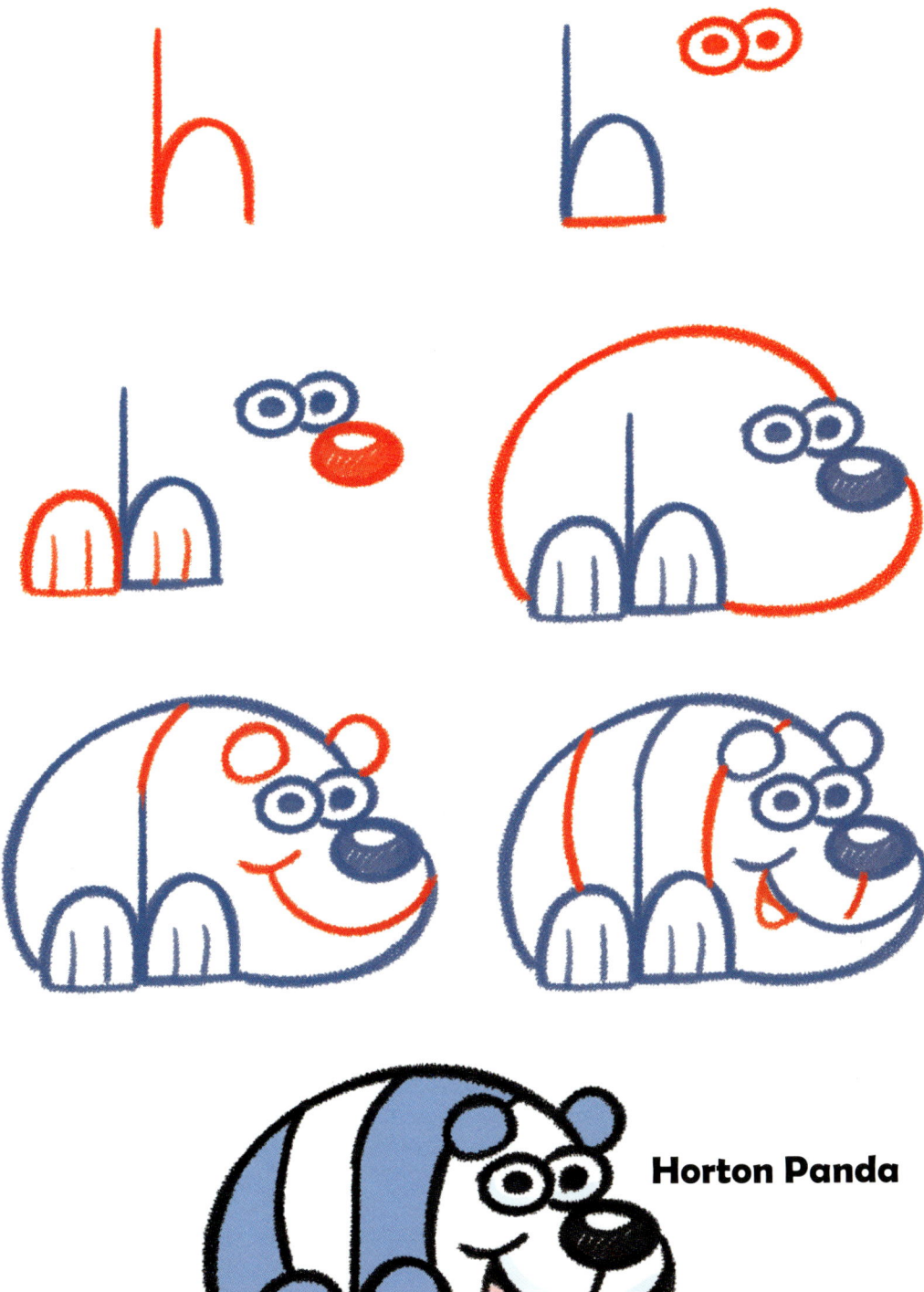

Horton Panda

Jason Seal

Mikey Snake

Ned Turtle

Orville Orangutan

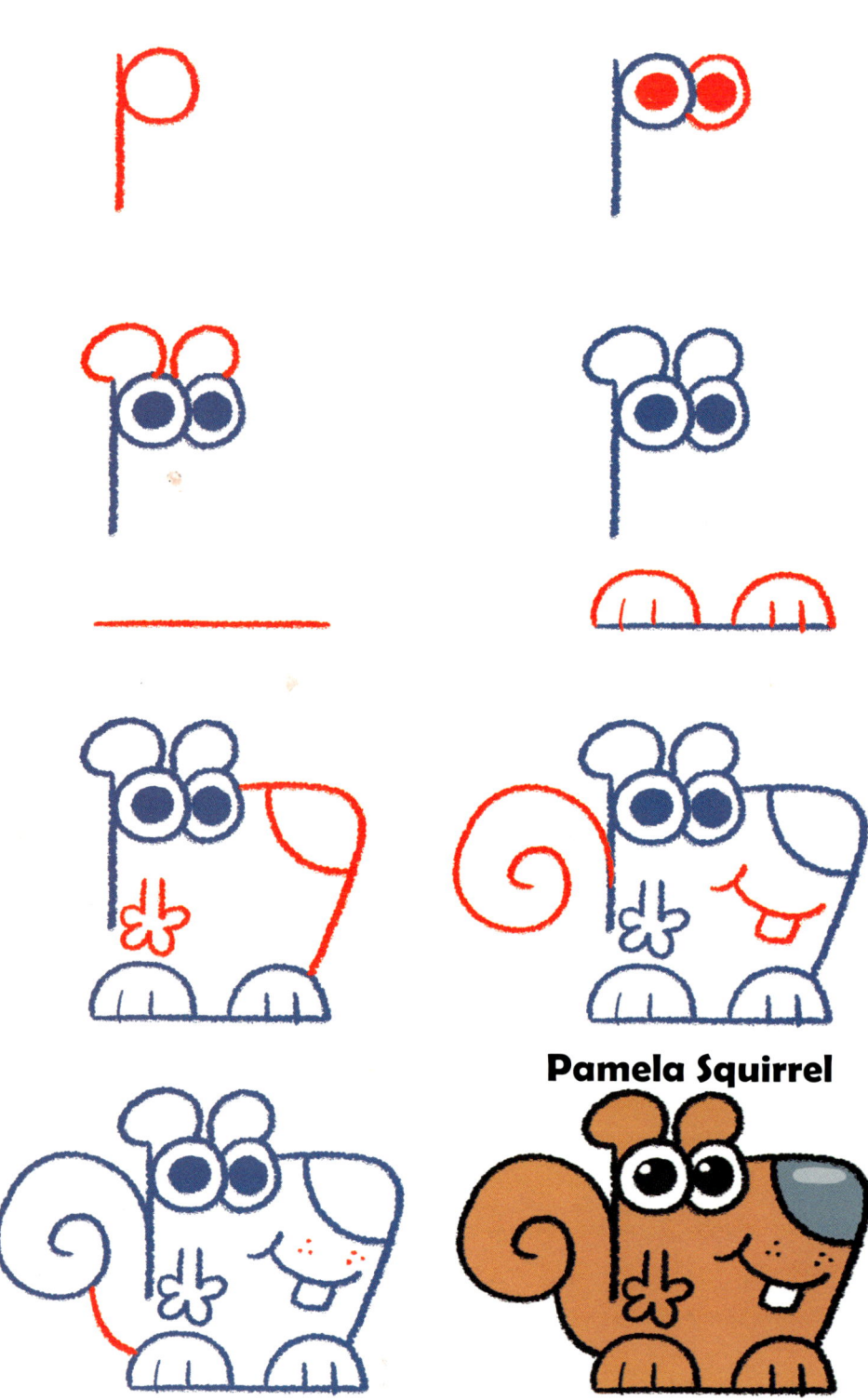

Pamela Squirrel

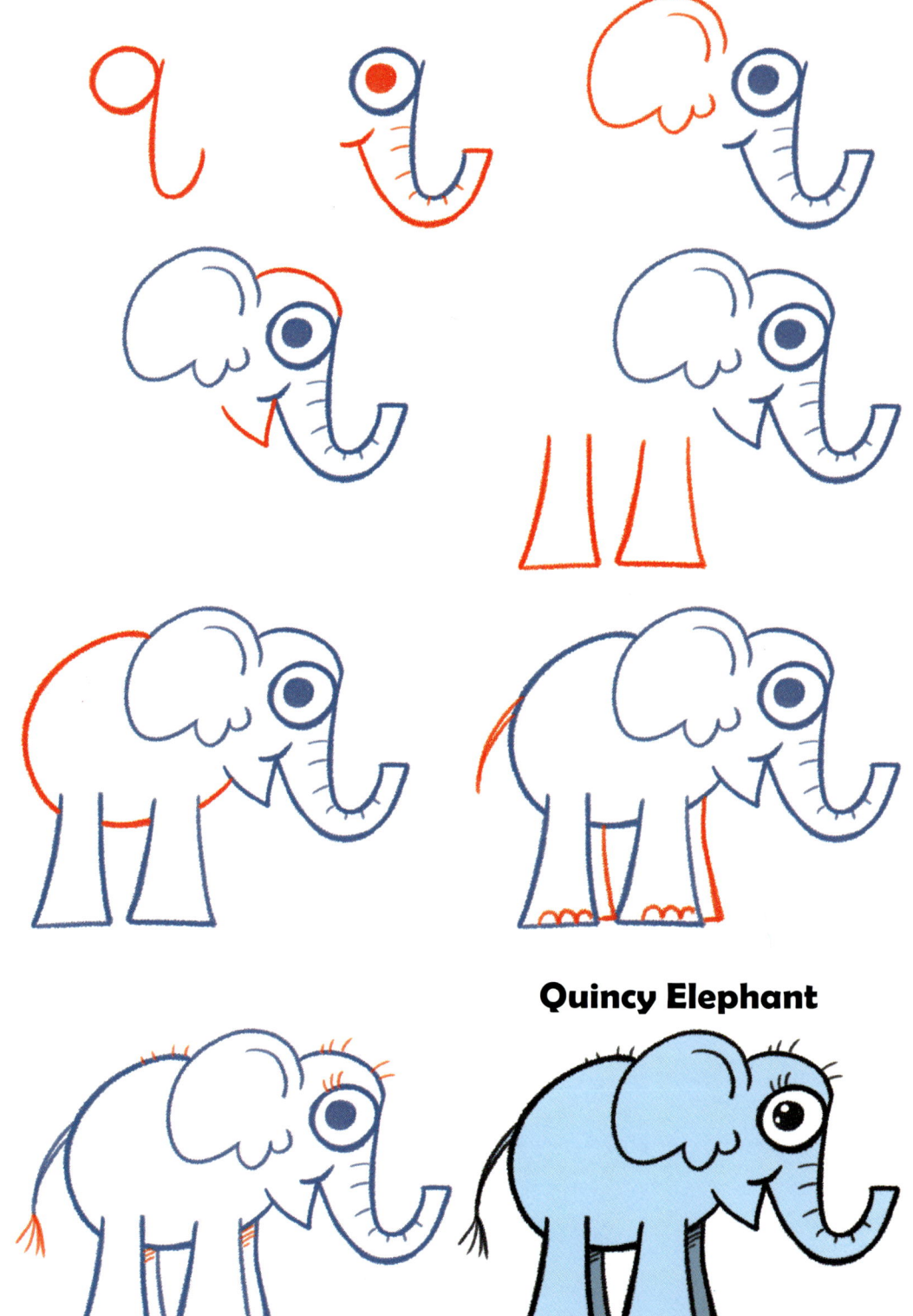
Quincy Elephant

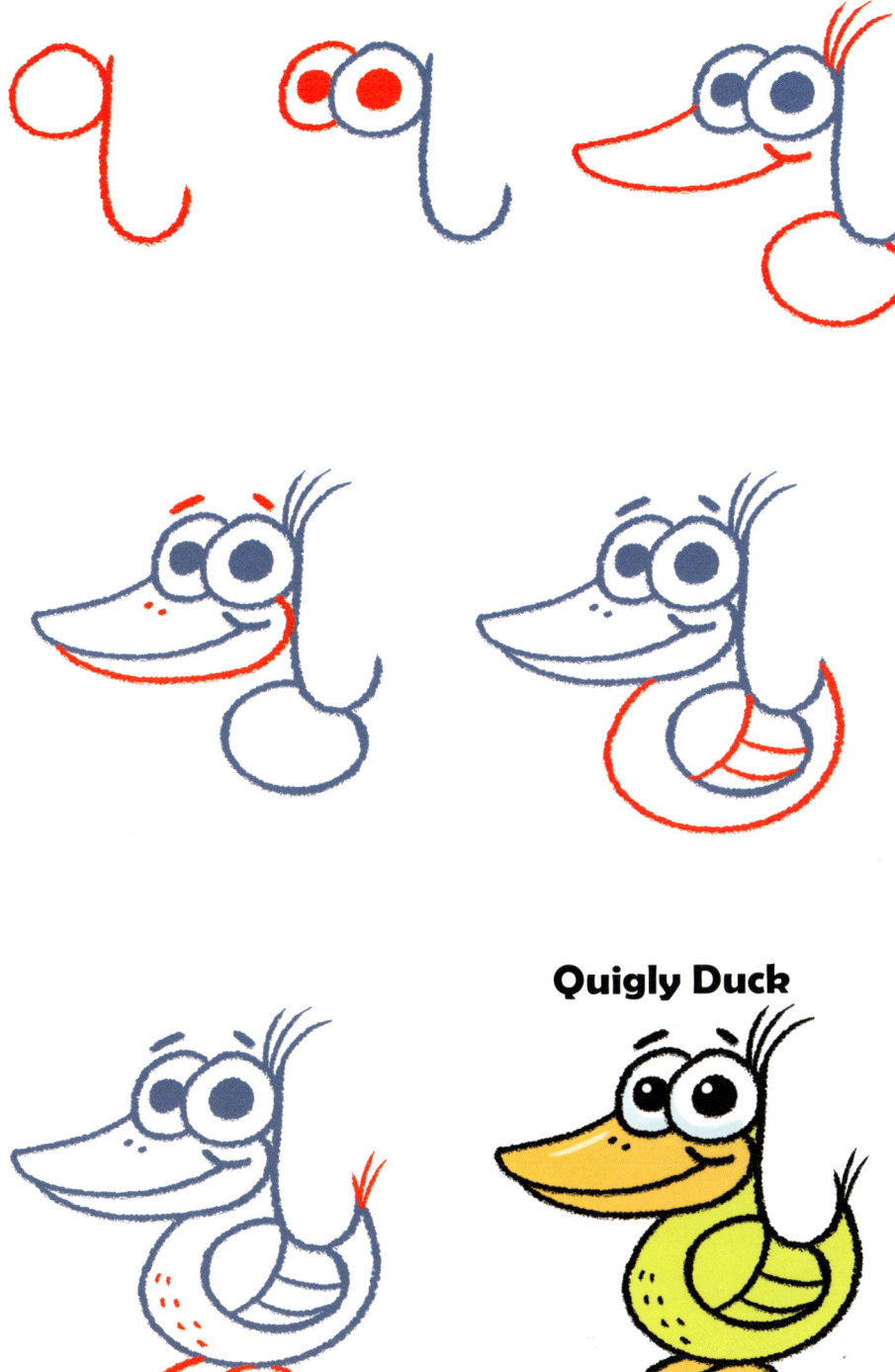

Quigly Duck

Roger Raccoon

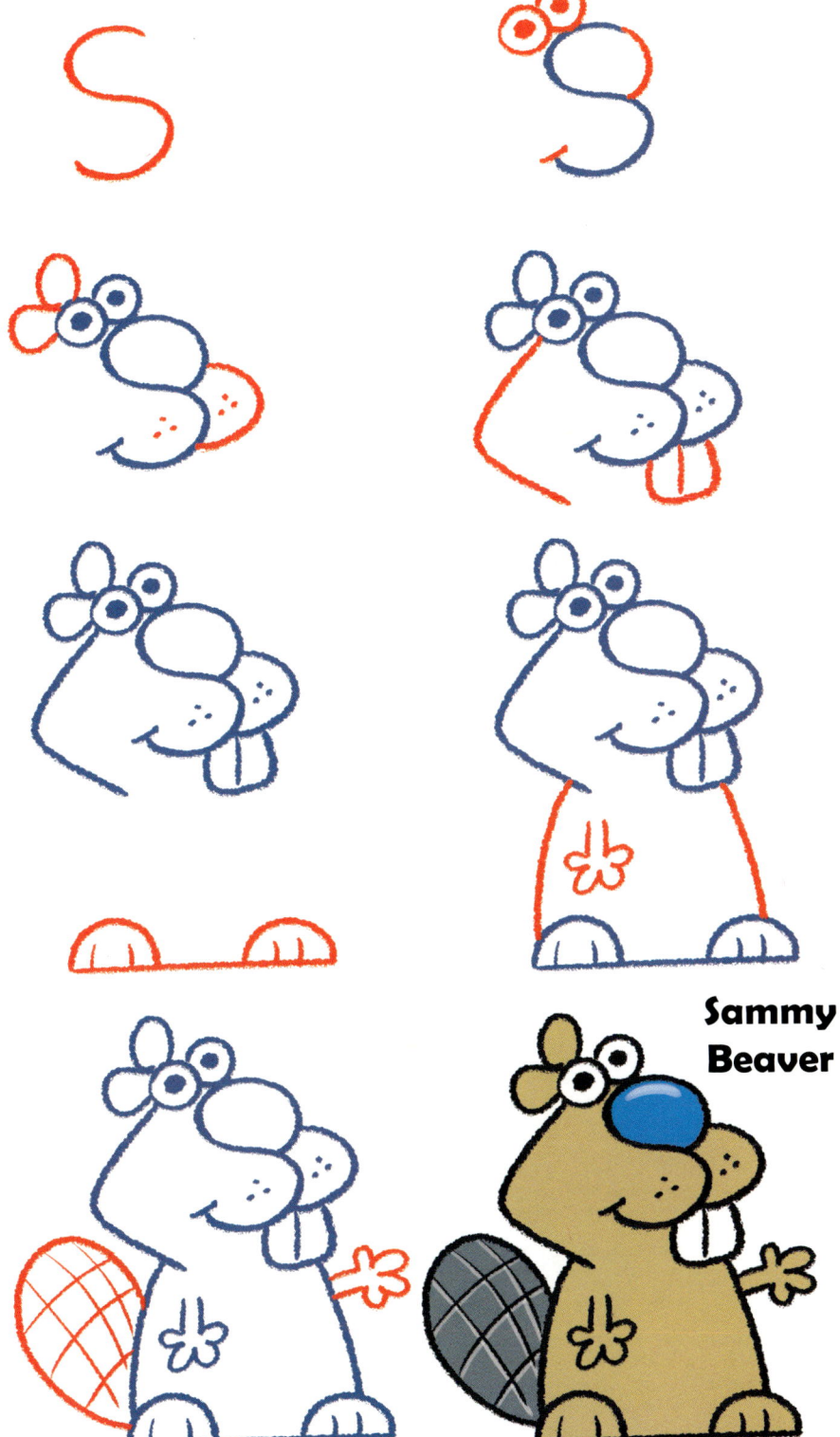

Sammy Beaver

Tilly Pig

Uggy Hippo

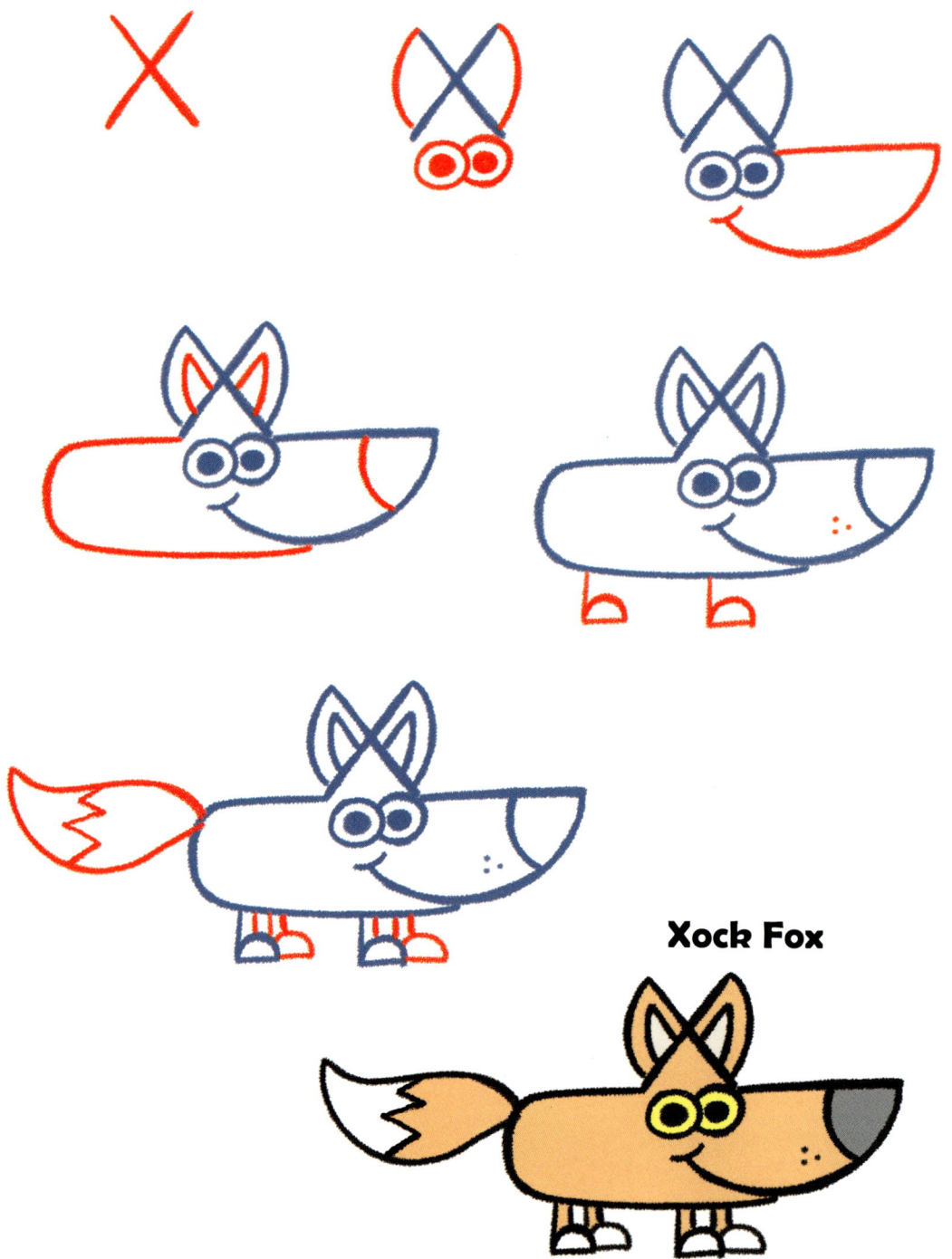

Xock Fox

Yuri Lion Cub

Visit Harptoons.com and watch how-to-draw videos, print off free coloring and activity pages, and create fun crafts. Email your drawings to art@harptoons.com and it might get featured in a Harptoons drawing video. All this and more at the greatest drawing site dedicated to getting young people drawing, creating and imagining.

Follow Harptoons on: